Non-Fungible Token (NFT)

Delve Into the World of NFTs Crypto Collectibles and How It Might Change Everything?

Vicky V. Choudhary

Foreword

Non-fungible Tokens (NFTs) have shaken the crypto world. Recently, we all might have heard the term 'Non-Fungible Tokens' or the 'NFTs'. May it be from news or games, or may it be from celebrities and artists, we all hear these terms quite frequently. Well, as a newbie, we did become curious and asked ourselves, "What is this craze of NFTs? Why is the world going insanely crazy about it?" Well, no need to worry? This book is all about answering your queries in the best comfortable way. NFTs are paving the way for future innovation with their unique properties. This book helps you understand the world of NFT crypto collectibles. It explains the NFT Ecosystem as well. It further explains how to buy, sell, and trade them. The book further discusses various aspects associated with the NFT Ecosystem.

Enjoy your reading.

Have a good time ahead.

Table of Contents

Chapter 1 Introduction to NFTs   9

What is exactly Non-Fungible Token (NFT)?   10

Chapter 2 Understanding Tokens   12

Let Us Understand What are Tokens?   12

Significance of Tokens   13

Chapter 3 Fungible and Non-Fungible   15

Understanding the term 'Fungibility'   15

Understanding Non-Fungibility   16

Comparison between Fungible and Non-Fungible
Tokens   17

Characteristics that set fungible and non-fungible
tokens apart   19

Chapter 4 Importance of NFTs   25

Chapter 5 Background of NFTs   27

Who created the first NFT?   27

The History of Non-Fungible Tokens   27

Chapter 6 Technical Details of the NFT

Ecosystem   33

Technical steps involved in NFT creation   33

Technical Components of NFTs   34

Chapter 7 Protocols & Token Standards   38

Token Standards   38

Ethereum Token Standards   39

Tezos Token Standards   40

Chapter 8 Security in NFTs   43

Re- entrant attack   43

Blockchain-related issue   44

Spoofing   44

Tampering   45

Denial Of Service Attack   45

Lost control over execution   46

Information leakage   46

Chapter 9 Applications of NFTs   47

Chapter 10 Challenges in the NFT System   51

Chapter 11 Marketplaces of NFTs   55

Chapter 12 Wallets Used in NFTs Transactions

59

Chapter 13 Creating, Buying and Selling

NFTs   **61**

Creating and Funding Your Account   61

Buying NFT   61

How to Create and Sell NFTs   62

How Are NFTs Created?   62

How Much Does It Cost?   63

Who Can Make An NFT?   64

The Process of Selling NFTs   64

Chapter 14 Future of the NFTs   **66**

Summary   **68**

References   **69**

Chapter 1
Introduction to NFTs

The non-fungible token has attracted a lot of attention as one of the most interesting and revolutionary blockchain innovations available to developers and enterprises. Non-fungible tokens (NFTs) are revolutionizing the way we own digital assets.

With the advancement of technology and the global pandemic, the digital world has undergone tremendous transformation. Digital investments and digital currencies are two examples of such transformations brought about by the new digital environment. Cryptocurrencies have grown into a large sector, resulting in an increase in the number of investors eager to participate in these digital assets and crypto-currencies across the country. The digital revolution has resulted in an open presentation of all information on the internet. People who are completely unaware of the ownership and authorship of the works shown online have had a negative impact on the production and creativity of original artists on the digital platform. Artists and creators are left with only a fraction of the value of their work due to a lack of security and authenticity.

This is what NFTs are designed to fix; they reflect ownership of a one-of-a-kind item that is then linked to a token via the blockchain. As the year 2020 approaches the mainstream art world, the market for NFTs has risen to over 338 million dollars, up from 41 million dollars in 2018. In the NFT market, a new generation of traders has emerged, consisting of digitally native individuals with established reputations and money who are willing to participate in asset classes outside of conventional asset markets. Millions of artists and investors around the world have recently become interested in non-fungible tokens as their popularity has grown.

What is exactly Non-Fungible Token (NFT)?

Non-Fungible Token is abbreviated as NFT. The word non-fungible refers to the non-interchangeable element of it, emphasizing its uniqueness. The term token refers to how it is considered as a transferable digital asset (art, music, in-game item) that is stored on a blockchain and tracked via smart contracts.

NFTs can be thought of as a proof of ownership of crypto or physical goods on a digital marketplace powered by blockchain technology, where blockchain refers to a digital ledger that keeps track of transactions in the form of a decentralized database. NFTs are defined as a cryptographic asset on the blockchain that consists of unique identification codes and metadata that allows them to be distinguished from one another. They are not interchangeable by definition. They can't be replaced by another identical creation, therefore. They seek to provide ownership of a specific digital work by limiting the unlimited quantity of digital creation. They are one-of-a-kind digital tokens that may be bought, sold, and traded between individuals on digital networks. These precious NFTs have been used by a variety of artists all around the world. They sell their creations in the form of art while retaining their copyrights.

Chapter 2
Understanding Tokens

Let Us Understand What are Tokens?

The definition of tokens is the most important factor to consider when determining the differences between fungible and non-fungible tokens. Tokens are a visible or tactile representation of a sensation, truth, or characteristic in the real world. In daily life, people come across a variety of tokens. A hotel key card, for example, is confirmation that you paid for a room at the hotel. The office ID card serves as verification of work. A driving license, on the other hand, certifies that an individual has completed the appropriate training to drive in their nation. As a result, a token also symbolizes a specific entity in the crypto world.

The token can be used to store money, voting rights, stakes, or anything else. Surprisingly, a token is not limited to a single function and can be used to address a variety of functions in its local ecosystem. A token could be used to represent a company's utility or value. In a public sale, the corporation can sell the tokens to investors.

Significance of Tokens

A token isn't limited to a single function and can be used for a variety of things in its original ecosystem. The following are examples of functions: Tokens can be used as entry points for blockchain applications, and users will require tokens to use the decentralized app.

- Individuals' qualifications for possessing specific voting rights could potentially be represented via tokens. EOS blockchain coins, for example, can be used to vote on block makers.

- Tokens can also be useful for enhancing the user experience of their owners. Enhancement tokens for user experience can help improve user experience within the confines of a certain context. For example, in the case of the Brave web browser, users with BAT or other Brave-related tokens may be able to augment their customer experience by using their tokens to add adverts or other attention-based services related to the Brave platform.

- The use of tokens as currency also helps to distinguish fungible from non-fungible tokens. Tokens can be used as a store of value for internal and external transactions within a certain ecosystem, and they can also be used to create a new type of monetary system that includes digital assets.

- The exchange of value is another important use of tokens. In fact, in the blockchain ecosystem, tokens have typically been utilized for value exchange. As a result, tokens may be useful in the development of an application's internal economic system.
- It's also worth considering the use of tokens as a means of identifying who owns a specific business. Tokens can indicate ownership of something unique to a single user, and this use lays the groundwork for the dispute over fungible vs non-fungible tokens.

Chapter 3
Fungible and Non-Fungible Tokens

Understanding the term 'Fungibility'

To figure out what an NFT is, we must first comprehend the concept of fungibility. The term may appear sophisticated, yet it is a straightforward concept that we can apply to our daily lives.

A fungible item, at its most basic level, is one that can be swapped for another of the same categorization or description. Because each fungible unit is fundamentally identical, they can be swapped out. A wonderful example of a fungible asset is currency. Both your dollar bill and a dollar bill found on the ground are worth one dollar. Fungible goods/assets are divisible as well as interchangeable. This means they can be multiplied or divided without affecting the item's core essence. A dollar can be divided into any number of coins totaling 100 cents and yet represent the same amount of money.

Another important characteristic of fungibility is that minor physical changes between fungible items have no effect on their perceived or acknowledged value: When you try to use a banknote to pay for something, the serial number has no bearing on the face value, and it has no effect on their utility. In a store, a clean new $20 bill from the ATM will buy just as much as one that has been crumpled, tattered, and passed through countless hands for a decade. When it comes to fungible things, each unit is produced equal in the end.

Understanding Non-Fungibility

Non-fungible items are those that are not directly interchangeable or replaceable. Non-fungible goods, unlike fungible assets like Bitcoin, are distinguished by their unique, verifiable identity, provable scarcity, and indivisibility. Non-fungibility is linked to identification in various ways, whether it's the identity of the item, its owner, or its creator.

When something is non-fungible, each unit has its own distinct identity, which has an impact on its basic value. Differences in appearance, rarity, utility, and a variety of other characteristics have a direct impact on a unit's identity, and thus its value. Take the following non-fungible item as an example. A genuine artwork by a well-known artist is more valuable than a copy of the same painting.

Comparison between Fungible and Non-Fungible Tokens

Without a question, blockchain is the best technology for managing various forms of digital assets. Its immutability and security characteristics make it excellent for managing digital assets. It is hard to write any unique information to fungible tokens, which are the most often used ones in blockchain until now.

On the other hand, cryptographic tokens are one-of-a-kind. They could be ideal preferences since they can store information rather than value. Non-fungible tokens are ones that are created on Ethereum and adhere to ERC standards such as ERC-721. As a result, it's evident that the distinction between fungible and non-fungible tokens stems from the importance placed on data storage. Let's start with the distinction between fungible and non-fungible tokens.

The ability of any fungible entity to be interchanged with another asset or good of equal value is referred to as fungibility. Currency and money are the most common instances of fungible assets. For example, a $5 bill in one person's possession has the same value as a $5 bill in another person's possession. Similarly, two $5 dollars from one person are worth the same as a single $10 bill from another.

Another example of a fungible asset is gold. This is because one ounce of gold in one country has the same value as one ounce of gold in another. The dispute between fungible vs non-fungible tokens stems from the fact that fungibility is written into the code of Bitcoin and other cryptocurrencies. A fungible good is standardized, and fungible goods' units have no distinctiveness.

NFTs are a one-of-a-kind token version that cannot be exchanged for other tokens. NFT has distinct characteristics that plainly imply limitations when replacing or trading it with an identical token.

Non-fungible tokens are distinct from cryptocurrencies in that they lack intrinsic value. In fact, the non-fungible tokens get their value from the assets or things they represent. NFTs use a variety of token standards and implement various sorts of smart contracts. Non-fungible tokens are regarded as cutting-edge instruments for creating a blockchain-based virtual economic environment.

Characteristics that set fungible and non-fungible tokens apart

Interchangeability

Fungible tokens, as you may have guessed, are totally interchangeable with one another. Fiat currencies are the most well-known example of fungible assets. To pay for specific items, you can transfer fungible assets from one owner to another. Exchanging fungible assets, on the other hand, has no meaning because they have the same worth. Fungible tokens are commonly used for payment and balance tracking.

One notable example of a real blockchain use case for fungible tokens is the linking of tokens to an organization's account balance in a specific payment account. As a result, token transfers could be used to fulfil payments. Users can also do periodic netting and settlement by accessing the resulting token balances.

Value Transfer

Another interesting point is between fungible and non-fungible tokens, which relates to the fact that each account keeps track of its balance based on the tokens it owns. By utilizing direct transactions or swap procedures, it is simple to transfer tokens to other Ethereum accounts. Token transfers debit the source account in the same way as bank transfers do. Simultaneously, a credit of the same amount is applied to the recipient account.

When comparing fungible and non-fungible tokens, it's clear that non-fungible tokens, or NFTs, offer a distinct value proposition. NFTs are one-of-a-kind tokens, and each one has its own unique ID for distinguishing it from other tokens in the same smart contract. Because each token is treated differently, each non-fungible token has a unique owner. As a result, their values may change.

Certain NFTs can represent one-of-a-kind tributes with a proven scarcity. As a result, NFTs are in high demand, with more buyers and higher value than those expressing common features. Furthermore, NFTs may be used to facilitate both ownership transfer and trading.

The assignment of a non-fungible token to a real estate property is one of the most noteworthy use cases. After paying off the mortgage, users can transfer NFTs from the bank's Ethereum account to the house owner's Ethereum account. As a result, it presents a new type of use case for blockchain in the real estate market.

Token standards are the next key thing to consider when distinguishing between fungible and non-fungible tokens. If you want to build a healthy ecosystem, you should build decentralized apps on top of Ethereum that can communicate with one another seamlessly. Can you find various smart contract structures in two different tokens, such as Token Beta and Token Alpha, on the other hand? For the interaction between the two tokens, developers must analyze both contracts.

Furthermore, developers must lay out the precise methods by which tokens can communicate with one another. This factor, however, does not help with scalability. It will be tough to narrow down all conditions and qualifications for assuring that transfers can proceed via all tokens if there are 100 different tokens with 100 separate smart contracts.

As a result, a large number of sophisticated calculations for token transactions may be encountered. As a result, token standards emerged as a viable option for distinguishing between fungible and non-fungible tokens. As a result, the choice to standardize the rules regulating the underlying architecture of tokens is unquestionably a yardstick for distinguishing fungible from non-fungible tokens.

<u>Fungible Tokens Use ERC-20</u>

The precise collection of rules is known as ERC-20, and ERC stands for 'Ethereum Request for Comment.' ERC-20 is built on the foundations of totalSupply, approve, allowance, balanceOf, transfer, and transferFrom. For ERC-20 tokens, these are the required rules and functions.

Tokens, on the other hand, could have the three possible attributes listed below. A symbol, a token name, and a decimal up to 18 are among the features. The ERC-20 is a fungible standard because of these properties. As a result of the standards, fungible tokens are required to have the following attributes, which determine their place in the fungible vs non-fungible token dispute.

Tokens of the same type that are fungible can be used to replace one another. Fungible token governance is governed by similar fundamental rules. Fungible tokens are easily divided, allowing people to pay back a bigger amount with smaller fractions.

<u>Non-Fungible Tokens Use ERC-721</u>

The constraints of ERC-20, on the other hand, create significant conflicts. As a result, the ERC-721 token standard was created. The ERC-721 token standard may be used in the development of non-fungible tokens. Surprisingly, the ERC-721 token standard is very similar to the ERC-20 token standard in terms of functionality. The following are the primary reasons for the similarities between ERC-20 and ERC-721.

Without needing to master a slew of new skills, developers may quickly make the switch. The experience of keeping tokens in regular wallets and trading them on exchanges may be improved. The ERC-721 interface has two different methods with different functions, such as tranferFrom and ownerOf. The ownerOf function is used to find out who owns a token. The transferFrom function can be used to transfer token ownership.

Non-fungible and fungible tokens are clearly correct on their own terms. The comparison of fungible vs non-fungible tokens is an important factor that will shape the future of the blockchain ecosystem. Non-fungible tokens have a clear benefit over fungible tokens in terms of security and immutability. During the asset tokenization process, users can contribute additional information and context for the metadata.

However, due to its newness, users may have difficulties trusting non-fungible tokens. On the contrary, they are gaining traction in the blockchain ecosystem, with notable uses in gaming and art. As the argument between fungible versus non-fungible tokens heats up, new developments have the potential to make a significant impact.

Chapter 4
Importance of Non-Fungible Tokens

A non-fungible token (NFT) is distinct. It can represent any digital asset on a blockchain, such as Ethereum, Solana, Flow, Tezos, and so on. This makes it scarce, demonstrable, and precious. The introduction of NFTs has offered a new platform for artists and creators to showcase their creations or collections. As a result, a revolution is paving the way for artists to create and market their work, while collectors have complete transparency into the authenticity and provenance of their purchases.

NFT assets can be digital art, collectibles, a creative extension of music, a synergy of all three, or completely new and uncharted compositions. Using NFTs, creators continue to push the boundaries of creativity, customizing them in new and unique ways.

Many people are surprised that they can capture screenshots of the NFT without having to buy it. This is correct. However, they would be unable to sell it for the same price as the original. Every time the NFT changes hands on the secondary market, the new owner and the price paid are immediately recorded on the blockchain, which is a decentralized digital ledger of transactions that no one can change and that everyone can view. The notion is that by making these certificates of authenticity publicly viewable online, NFTs can ensure the origin of any item to which they are linked.

The fundamental item you're purchasing is code that takes the form of images. You're purchasing art in a different format. You're not a believer in the image. You're purchasing the image's property rights. By design, NFTs are tools that artists can use to verify their work without having to deal with the legacy art world's typical machinations (provenance). NFTs allow artists the freedom to determine their own rates for their creations - and control of their secondary market - thereby democratizing access to new marketplaces for artists all over the world, thanks to their ability to generate scarcity of digital work.

Chapter 5
Background of NFTs

Who created the first NFT?

The history of NFTs began on May 3rd, 2014. Kevin McCoy created the original NFT artwork. He came up with the name 'Quantum' for his non-fungible token. This was prior to the emergence of the bitcoin art market. A pixelated image of an octagon filled with objects like circles, arcs, and other shapes makes up Quantum. Each has the same central point, with larger shapes around smaller ones and hypnotically throbbing in vivid hues.

The History of Non-Fungible Tokens

Various cultural phenomena inspired the CryptoArt category. CryptoPunks, Rare Pepe, and CryptoKitties were among them. These works of 'art' became famous as a result of viral network effects and the willingness to spend significant sums of money to own them.

Colored Coins (2012-2013)

This is a long story that involves many persons, artists, and projects. The concept of NFTs arose from what is known as a 'colored coin.' It was first distributed on the Bitcoin blockchain between 2012 and 2013. Colored coins are tokens on the blockchain that represent real-world assets and may be used to establish ownership of any asset, from precious metals to cars to real estate, and even equities and bonds. The original concept was to leverage the Bitcoin network to store assets such as digital collectibles, coupons, real estate, company shares, and more. They were touted as innovative technology and provided raw possibilities for future usage.

Counterparty (2014)

Counterparty was founded in 2014 by Robert Dermody, Adam Krellenstein, and Evan Wagner. It was a financial platform for peer-to-peer transactions. It was an open-source internet protocol built on the Bitcoin blockchain that was distributed. Counterparty allowed users to generate assets and had a decentralized exchange, allowing them to build their own trading currencies. It featured a plethora of ideas and potential, including meme trading without the risk of counterfeiting.

Spells of Genesis on Counterparty (2015)

In April 2015, Counterparty worked with the Spells of Genesis crew. The creators of the Spells of Genesis game were the first to use Counterparty to issue in-game assets onto a blockchain. They were also among the first to conduct an initial coin offering (ICO). The creators contributed in the development of Counterparty. They achieved this by establishing their own in-game money, BitCrystals.

Trading Cards on Counterparty (2016)

In August 2016 new trends began to emerge. Counterparty teamed up with Force of Will. It was a popular trading card game. They launched their cards on the Counterparty platform. Force of Will was the 4th ranked card game in North America according to sales volume. First three were Pokemon, Yu-Gi-Oh and Magic. Force of Will had no prior blockchain or cryptocurrency experience before. Their entrance into the ecosystem signaled the value of putting such assets on a blockchain.

Rare Pepes on Counterparty (2016)

Memes first appeared on the blockchain in 2016. On the Counterparty platform, memes began to proliferate. People began to contribute items to the 'Rare Pepes' craze. Rare Pepes is a meme featuring a one-of-a-kind frog character. The character has garnered a considerable fan base over the years. The character was inspired by Pepe the Frog. It has subsequently become one of the most popular memes on the internet. By early 2017, Ethereum was gaining traction. Rare Pepes began to be exchanged as well. Jason Rosenstein, the founder of Portion, collaborated with Louis Parker. They held the world's first live Rare Pepe auction. It took place at the first-ever Rare Digital Art Festival. The Rare Pepe Wallet gave birth to CryptoArt. It was the first time that artists from all around the world could submit and sell their own work. It was also the first time that digital art had intrinsic worth.

Cryptopunks and Cryptokitties (2017)

The demand for Rare Pepes had increased. John Watkinson and Matt Hall co-founded Larva Labs. They also used Ethereum's blockchain to create one-of-a-kind characters. There would be no two similar characters, and there would be a character limit of 10,000. A Bitcoin experiment from the 1990s inspired Cryptopunks. It's a hybrid between ERC721/ERC20.

By utilising ERC721, CryptoKitties NFTs got off to a quick start. They're a virtual cat adoption, breeding, and trading game built on the Ethereum blockchain. They gained a lot of attention. CNBC and Fox News both featured them. CryptoKitties were created by Axiom Zen, a Vancouver-based company. It was quite well-liked. It acquired money from major investors as a result of the increased user base. Axiom Zen spun off CryptoKitties, and Dapper Labs was born.

The NFT Explosion (2018 Onwards)

Between 2018 and 2021, NFTs slowly moved into public awareness. It then exploded into mainstream adoption in early 2021.

The crypto world was taken by storm by the ostensibly underlying movement. It has gradually evolved into more mainstream art. Valentine's Day 2018 marked a turning point in this journey. Kevin Abosch, an artist, collaborated with GIFTO on a philanthropic auction. The relationship resulted in a $1 million transaction for The Forever Rose, a stunning piece of CryptoArt.

Mr. Abosch kept raising the stakes. In a project named 'IAMA Coin,' he began combining the Ethereum blockchain with his blood. Abosch isn't the only artist who has embraced this fascinating way of expression. It's steadily gaining appeal among artists eager to test their creative limits.

Traditional asset transfer tactics are inefficient and liquid, whereas non-traditional asset transfer markets are more efficient and liquid. On the internet, a slew of new platforms has popped up. Each has its own unique features that appeal to both producers and collectors. The reduction of centralized fees, which might be as much as 40% for traditional art dealers and auction houses, is the primary source of disruption. Opensea is widely regarded as the world's largest marketplace for art, music, domain names, collectibles, and trading cards. Mintable's platform is designed to make the minting process as simple as possible for creators. Other services, such as Niftex, let users to purchase fractions of NFTs or shards. These are ERC20 tokens that represent a portion of the entire NFT.

Chapter 6
Technical Details of the NFT Ecosystem

This chapter discusses the technical details of the NFTs system.

Technical steps involved in NFT creation

The process of developing and then trading an NFT consists of five major steps. These steps are as follows.

- The actual creation of art is the first stage. This art can be in the form of an image, digital art, audio file, or other medium.

- The file is uploaded by the NFT creator. A description and title are written by the creator. The creator then decides on the royalty percentage they want on the resale.

- The information is subsequently entered into the database of the exchange where the NFT is listed by the owner. This database exists in its own right, separate from the blockchain. The owner may also save the data in the blockchain. They will, however, be charged for gas.

- When a transaction is sent to a smart contract, it is received. The owner's signature and the hash of the NFT data are both included in this transaction.

- At this point, the NFT is minted, and the trading process begins. When the smart contract confirms the transaction, the minting procedure is complete. The NFT is now stored in the blockchain at a unique address for the rest of its life.

On the blockchain, the NFTs are stored. It is possible to keep track of who was the original owner. Because the transactions are stored in blocks, this is the case. These blocks are linked to the next, resulting in an immutable long history. When a new transaction interacts with a smart contract, such as when an NFT is generated or traded, the NFT metadata are added to the new block. This is done after the new owner's information has been verified. As a result, the owner has a secure property right.

Technical Components of NFTs

The technological components of the NFT system are discussed further.

Blockchain

A blockchain is an immutable increasing list of records linked together via encryption. It is decentralized. It is administered via a peer-to-peer network of nodes and will eventually be utilized as a publicly distributed ledger. Its beginnings can be traced back to 1991. This is when Stuart Haber and W. Scott Stornetta created a cryptographically secure chain of blocks. No one in this chain could tamper with the timestamps of the papers. It has received numerous enhancements.

The year 2008 saw the beginning of bitcoin. It was at this time that the blockchain saw its first application in the real world. Bitcoin, unlike other efforts, was able to tackle the problem of double-spending. Blockchains employ a number of different consensus processes. Proof of work (PoW), proof of stake (PoS), and many others are among them. Each has advantages and disadvantages. A blockchain has numerous real-world applications. Cryptocurrencies, smart contracts, decentralized finance, and video games are just a few examples. Others include supply chains, healthcare, domain names, and NFTs.

The majority of NFT projects are hosted on the Ethereum blockchain. Because of its ERC721 and ERC1155 standards, this is the case. These specifications are more suited to hosting NFTs. This is also owing to the Ethereum blockchain's inclusion of solidity smart contracts. The Flow and Tezos blockchains are also worthy to be noticed.

Smart Contracts

In 1994, the first smart contract was established. Nick Szabo was the founder. He founded BitGold as well. A smart contract is a static or dynamic block of code. It includes the buyer's and seller's previously agreed-upon terms. The code is automatically executed after the agreement has been met. Scrypt enabled Bitcoin to implement simple smart contracts.

With the introduction of Ethereum and its solidity language, more complicated smart contracts are now conceivable. It should be highlighted that these gains come at the expense of decreased security and greater error proneness. Smart contracts have a wide range of applications. One such application is the elimination of the middleman as a payment route.

Web3 Wallet

A web3 wallet is a tool for interacting with web 3.0 apps, commonly known as the internet's third generation. The Web3 wallet can store both cryptocurrency and crypto assets such as NFTs. Metamask and Trust wallet are two instances of web3 wallets.

Address and Transaction

A blockchain address is a unique identifier. It is like an email address. It's made up of a specific number of alphanumeric characters. A pair of public and private keys are used to generate these characters. A blockchain address is a one-of-a-kind identification number. It enables the user to send and receive digital assets such as bitcoins. When delivering a crypto asset, the user must show ownership of the associated private key. Only the creator, who has a valid digital signature, is allowed to send the commodity or currency to another address.

Data Encoding

Converting data from one form to some other is called data encoding. It is employed to compress information with a view to save disk space or to extend for better resolution. In utmost blockchains hex values are used to encrypt transactions. In essence, an NFT holder holds a real hex cost signed with the aid of the original artist. This solves the challenge posed by way of the manner of copying an NFT and claiming it to belong to themselves. This is due to the fact a fake possessor doesn't have the original hex inked with the aid of the author. The fake person can't claim their right on that particular NFT. This makes NFT special.

Chapter 7
Protocols & Token Standards

A protocol is required to efficiently and securely store and trade NFTs. A protocol is a decentralized ledger with an ever-increasing amount of records. It also has a peer-to-peer network for exchanging data. NFTs are supported by a significant variety of blockchain systems. Among them are Ethereum, Tezos, and Flow. The first NFT was created using the ERC721 standard.

On Ethereum, the proof of work consensus (PoW) process is still in use. As a result, a lot of energy is consumed. Therefore, specialists are working to establish proof of stake (PoS). This is a particularly energy-efficient consensus process. It is supposed to be better for the environment. The other blockchain systems mentioned above already use PoS. They are getting up to Ethereum in terms of market share.

Token Standards

To describe what the token can perform, a token standard is required. A Token standard establishes a set of attributes and regulations that a project must adhere to in order to communicate with exchanges and wallets. There are numerous standards for various protocols. There are several standards even within a protocol. The token standards of various protocols, such as Ethereum and Tezos, will be discussed here.

Ethereum Token Standards

There are numerous token specifications on Ethereum. The most important ones are described further down.

ERC-20

It is the most used Ethereum based standard by most of the Ethereum based projects. ERC-20 tokens are also called 'fungible' tokens as these tokens are interchangeable. Each token is worth the same amount as the other. Some examples of these are governance tokens and stable coins.

ERC-721

This is a non-interchangeable token standard. It's a one-of-a-kind piece of property. ERC-721 tokens are a whole asset that cannot be divided. A certificate or a tokenized item are two examples. Contract values are unique to each ERC-721 token. These values could be data about the ownership and identity of a tokenized real-world asset like a house.

Immutability, ownership transparency, and security are all good points for ERC-721s. Despite their complete flexibility in the production of a token, this is possible. Non-fungible is a term used to describe ERC-721 tokens. They are non-fungible tokens because they are one-of-a-kind (NFTs).

ERC-1155

In terms of non-fungibility, the ERC-721 token standard is excellent. However, when transferring a large number of tokens at once, they prove to be slow and inefficient.
The ERC-1155 token standard is useful in this situation. Enjin designed it. Unique digital NFTs are provided by this standard. When compared to ERC-721, it allows for much faster batch transfers of multiple tokens. It places a strong emphasis on a true "multi-token" strategy. ERC-1155 is often characterized to as a "next-generation multi-token standard."

Tezos Token Standards

In Tezos, there are three token specifications. TIPZ is the Tezos Interoperability Proposal format.

FA1- TZIP 5 Abstract Ledger

FA1 Abstract Ledger initially lacked a clear interface. It was designed to address a market void for a basic abstract ledger. It was designed to be used as a component in applications that required the concept of a fungible asset. It satisfies the fundamental abstraction criteria and balances identities.

FA1 has a number of disadvantages. There is no explicit technique for documenting incoming transactions in contracts. Certain features that are commonly desired when executing a contract have been purposely left out. Finally, it makes no provision for the handling of additional contracts involving user payments.

FA1.2 - TZIP 7 Approvable Ledger

It's a new standard for interacting with smart contracts. FA1.2 is in charge of token transfers and spending authorizations from other accounts. It is very similar to the ERC-20. It carries out token transfer operations. Permissions to spend tokens from other accounts are implemented. It also connects identity to equilibrium. It also has the capacity to withstand attack vector vulnerabilities. This is a problem with the ERC-20 standard.

FA2- TZIP 12 Multi-Asset Interface

It was created so that Tezos developers wouldn't have to rely on token-specific standards. FA2 provides a unified token contract interface that supports a wider range of token types and implementations. FA2 doesn't care about tokens. This means that it uses a single standard to support both single-token and multi-token contracts. At all entry points, batch procedures are used. Multiple token transfers can now be carried out in a single atomic transaction.

Developers must handle common issues in accordance with this standard. Specifying the contract's token type is one such factor. FA2 has several benefits. It can handle a wide variety of token types and implementations. It accomplishes this by establishing a standard for a standardized token contract interface.

Token transfer rules are available in FA2. It supports a number of transfer authorization schemes that are resistant to ERC-20 attacks. FA2 is compatible with a wide range of standards. ERC-20, ERC-721, and ERC-1155 are examples of these. ERC-20 (fungible tokens) and ERC-721 (secured tokens) are the most popular (non-fungible tokens).

Chapter 8
Security in NFTs

The ecosystem for NFTs is still in its early stages. It still has a long way to go before reaching full maturity. As a result, the security risks associated with the NFT area must be taken into account. A number of dangers are described in greater detail.

Re- entrant attack

In computer science, a process is said to be re-entrant if it can be stopped in the middle of execution, restarted, and both runs completed successfully. A hacker's attack of this type can result in major vulnerabilities. The DAO hack was one such attack. In this instance, $70 million in Ether was taken. It's the most evident instance of this. The Ethereum Constantinople hard fork was postponed. This was done after a reentrancy issue was detected during the launch's final stages.

There are various options for putting a halt to this attack. The transmit() or transfer() functions should be used instead of the call.value() function. If no internal state changes occur following any transfer or external function call within the procedure, it is shielded from the re-entrancy vulnerability.

Blockchain-related issue

The possibility of a blockchain-based risk exists at all times. Consider the following illustration. The so-called "51 percent attack" is known to be vulnerable to blockchains that use proof-of-work for block creation. A person who controls 51 percent of a blockchain's hash rate has complete control over that blockchain. Proof-of-stake systems are vulnerable to a variety of threats. Fake stake attacks are one such example.

Spoofing

Spoofing occurs when a cybercriminal impersonates another person, corporation, or entity in order to gain power and carry out damaging operations. The attacker can obtain the original owner's private keys by exploiting the authentication weakness. The NFT can then be transferred to the attacker's wallet. Using a cold wallet and having a proper NFT smart contract verification are the best ways to combat this attack.

Tampering

It's when a hacker alters data with malevolent purpose. Even if NFTs are available on a blockchain, altering data after a transaction is challenging. Data stored outside of the blockchain, on the other hand, may be tampered with. As a result, it is recommended that a seller provide both the NFT and the hash data to the buyer at the time of exchange.

Denial Of Service Attack

In, denial-of-service (DoS) involves a network attack. A hostile attacker attempts to disrupt routine operations in order to make a server unavailable to its intended users. The NFT service is disrupted and accessibility is hampered by DoS attacks. Unauthorized users may take advantage of this. User actions are easily accessible thanks to the blockchain. Legitimate users are free to use the information as they see fit. Human error does not result in the loss of data resources.

Outside of the blockchain, DoS can be used to attack centralized web programmes or raw data. The NFT service may become inaccessible as a result of this. Recently, a novel hybrid blockchain architecture was designed. It solves availability concerns with two algorithms and a weak consensus mechanism.

Lost control over execution

Malicious assaults may expose latent flaws in even fully functional smart contracts. They operate in a completely anonymous manner on the network. As a result, we are left with no choice but to terminate them. The contract owner's express stop option is called Emergency Stop. It's a fantastic approach. This can turn a vulnerable function or a whole intelligent contract dysfunctional.

Information leakage

When data is made available to unauthorized users, this is known as information leakage. The NFT system is transparent in terms of state information and smart contract instruction codes. Every observer has access to any state and its changes. Even if the user simply enters the NFT hash into the blockchain, malicious attackers can easily exploit the risk and transaction responsibility. Therefore, the NFT developer should utilize sophisticated contracts that protect the user's privacy rather than simple intelligent contracts.

Chapter 9
Applications of NFTs

NFTs have a wide range of applications. Various applications are further described.

Digital art

One of the first applications of an NFT was digital art. It has the advantage of providing better income collecting opportunities for digital artists. This is owing to the fact that royalty exists. On each trade of the specific NFT, it is paid to the creator. It also serves as confirmation of ownership, which adds value to the item. There are various successful NFTs that have been marketed as digital art. The most well-known is that of artist Beeple, whose digital painting was auctioned for $69 million in March 2021 at Christie's.

Gaming

NFT has the ability to revolutionize the game business. It is capable of effectively monetizing a player's time. As a result, the intended play to earn dynamic is made easier. The game's economics are set up in such a way that a good player is rewarded for improving their skills. In-game cryptocurrency is used to pay out the reward. In addition, gamers can construct their own types of NFTs. In-game collectibles, for which they will receive a royalty on resale, are one example. Some of the projects have been the most successful in this regard. Some notable projects in this field are Axie Infinity, CryptoKitties, and Decentraland.

Collectables

An NFT's core characteristic is uniqueness and proof of ownership. As a result, NFTs are a fantastic type of collectible. They also shield the owner from any infringement of his or her intellectual property rights. NBA Top Shots is one of the prominent NFT that has delved into this domain. NBA players' cards are marketed as NFTs in this. The CryptoKitties are another example. Images of cats are offered as NFT in this. These can be bred to generate even more distinctive CryptoKitties.

Fashion

Cryptography is used to connect physical goods, such as wearables, to the blockchain. Consider the following illustration. An NFT can be made out of a jacket. By scanning the QR code on the jacket, the owner can be identified.

Real estate

The growing real estate prices have made it impossible for small investors to enter the market. However, with the help of NFTs, new ways have been developed. Tokenization is used to purchase fractions of real estate in such advances. On the blockchain, the data is stored. This provides investors with very solid proof of ownership. The property can be rented out with the use of smart contracts. As a result, investors can earn a passive income based on their holdings and the smart contract regulations. As a result, the obstacles for small investors interested in the real estate market have been broken down.

Metaverse

The Metaverse is a collaborative virtual environment. People in Metaverse can engage in a wide range of digital activities. In general, it employs a number of techniques. The virtual environment is created using augmented reality and the Internet. The idea has been around for a long time. Blockchain has a promising future because of its rapid expansion. Blockchain provides a decentralized ecology in virtual online environments. Participants may be involved in this blockchain-based alternative for a number of reasons.

This can include games, the arts, commercial items, and virtual assets.

Users can also participate in the virtual economy. Structures such as offices can be leased to other parties in order to collect a debt. It may also be utilized to make one-of-a-kind creatures and sell them for rewards. Among the most noteworthy are Decentraland, my neighbor Alice, and a few more blockchain-based initiatives.

Chapter 10
Challenges in the NFT Ecosystem

The NFT ecosystem faces a variety of challenges and threats. These are the roadblocks that must be overcome to move forward. These difficulties are listed below and affect a wide range of areas of work.

High gas price

This is the charge that users must pay for all blockchain transactions. As the network becomes more overloaded, gas prices climb. As a result, the NFT exchanges are having a lot of trouble. The creation of an NFT collection is no longer feasible. Because every blockchain transaction demands the use of computing and storage resources, this charge is enforced.

Art Theft

This is a major flaw in the NFT system. Anyone with access to the blockchain might take someone else's artwork that hasn't been released on blockchain. They can claim ownership by converting it to an NFT.

Processing time

Transactions involving the minting or trading of NFTs proceed through a smart contract, which interacts with the blockchain. This has a low transaction per second right now. This slows down the processing and creates a negative user experience. Some of the new Proof of Stake (PoS) blockchains, such as Algorand, have mostly resolved this issue. However, there is still a long way to go.

Anonymity

Currently, the majority of NFT projects are built on Ethereum, Flow, and Tezos. They do not offer complete anonymity to their users. They offer pseudo-anonymity. Anyone may see every transaction from every wallet address. This covers the wallet balances as well. Bad actors, such as hackers, may exploit this knowledge. They may be able to gain access to some of these wallets. There are solutions available, such as zero-knowledge proofs. Multi-party signatures are already in the works. However, they have not been implemented on the majority of these blockchains.

Carbon footprint

We live in a period when environmental damage and energy crises are among the most serious issues confronting our world. Using computing resources to safeguard our digital work isn't considered as a priority in such a setting. It's even being chastised for expanding the carbon impact.

Legal issues

Many NFT exchanges do not have a KYC (know your customer) policy. NFTs trading entails commodity trading as well as cross-border transactions. Before investing any money in the area, it is critical to understand a country's regulatory attitude. Currently, the selling of NFTs is not regarded as a taxable event. This can lead to massive amounts of financial fraud in the system. As a result, governments should think about regulating and taxing. This is necessary in order to guard its population from any potential risk.

Storing NFT off-chain

The majority of NFT marketplaces now store digital art in a separate database. This isn't a blockchain database, therefore don't expect it to work. This is because storing an image or video file necessitates a large quantity of block space and computing power. As a result, you'll be saddled with a large gas bill. It has the potential to jam the network in the long run. As a result, minting NFTs is a very expensive process for customers. As a result, they merely save a cryptographic hash as an identity on the blockchain to avoid this. It is tethered to the token. Users of the NFT marketplace lack trust as a result of this method.

Chapter 11
Marketplaces of NFTs

You must follow specific measures if you want to learn how to buy NFT. First and foremost, one must determine where NFTs are sold. There are markets where you may buy and sell NFTs because it is a blockchain-based token. So, before we go any further, lets highlight some of the most popular markets.

You may purchase and sell NFTs on a number of different internet markets. However, not all marketplaces sell the same collectibles or works of art. As a result, you can buy a certain sort of collectable depending on the marketplace you pick. Most of these markets have a large selection of NFTs to choose from. However, each platform functions in a unique way. It's easy to become perplexed regarding where to acquire NFTs. The following are some of the markets where you may purchase and sell NFTs.

OpenSea

OpenSea is a fantastic Ethereum-powered NFT marketplace. Non-fungible tokens can be purchased using crypto. There are several collectibles available. Artwork to video games are examples of this. To utilise this platform, however, you must first obtain a blockchain wallet, such as Metamask. Many different blockchain wallets are supported by OpenSea. Metamask, Trust, Coinbase, Argent, and other similar services fall within this category. This is a popular venue for purchasing NFTs.

SuperRare

SuperRare is another excellent venue for purchasing NFTs. Every artwork in this gallery is one-of-a-kind. All tokens may be sold and purchased using respective systems. The Ethereum network is used by this platform. So, in order to purchase any goods from this site, you must first acquire Ether.

CryptoPunks

CryptoPunks is now one of the leading names in the industry. It differs from other NFT marketplaces in a few ways. In actuality, these are mostly photos with a resolution of 24 x 24 pixels. Algorithms are used to produce all of the photos automatically. The majority of these photos include punk-looking females and guys. However, certain objects are more uncommon, such as zombie punks or alien punks. Every punk has his or her own portfolio. You can examine their attributes, ownership status, and whether or not they are for sale in this portfolio.

This is comparable to CryptoKitties in the sense that each item is one-of-a-kind. Likewise, each punk is unique. You may buy punks, make bids on them, and then auction them off for a greater price on this marketplace.

Rarible

Rarible and OpenSea are quite similar. It participates actively in the digital transformation of the token-based blockchain. You may also produce, purchase, sell, and bid on art items in this marketplace. You may use this platform to construct an NFT and auction your digital assets. Those interested in purchasing these files can place a bid. That picture will be owned by the highest bidder. For selling purposes, you may also make many NFTs for a single picture. It's possible to resell it several times. Furthermore, you may be paid a commission on resales.

Sorare

Sorare is designed exclusively for soccer cards. This website allows you to purchase and sell limited-edition digital soccer cards. There are a lot of clubs available on the market.

If you enjoy soccer, Sorare is the right NFT marketplace for you. You may purchase soccer cards of your favorite players.

Chapter 12
Wallets Used in NFTs Transactions

Blockchain Wallets

You'll need a blockchain wallet that may potentially handle ERC standards like ERC-721 and ERC-1155. Both of them are designed specifically for NFTs. ERC-1155, on the other hand, is a relatively new standard. As a result, several popular wallets may still be unable to support it.

The following are some of the blockchain wallets that are mentioned. These wallets may be used to store NFTs and other cryptos in order to purchase NFT. These wallets are supported by the majority of NFT markets.

MetaMask

MetaMask is a well-known decentralized finance platform. The Ethereum network is used. In actuality, you may use this wallet as a browser extension. Metamask allows you to access your assets as well as other Ethereum-based coins.

You may also use MetaMask to access the test network if you're a blockchain developer. By providing users with an abstraction, MetaMask lowers the entry hurdles for those interested in Ethereum. This is also where you may keep your NFTs. Furthermore, the gadget stores and encrypts all of your private keys. You have access to the keys at any time and may accept or reject NFT sales.

Coinbase Wallet

Among the NFT platforms, the Coinbase wallet is another popular option. It works with multi-coins and other digital collectibles. It provides safe storage. There is one significant difference here. Instead of utilizing solely addresses, you may use your Coinbase wallet name to make transactions. In actuality, it is available as a separate app. This makes it even more convenient for you to use because you can download the app on your mobile devices.

Chapter 13
Creating, Buying and Selling NFTs

Creating and Funding Your Account

You can open an account with any NFT marketplace. You must establish a connection to your blockchain wallet. The majority of NFTs are Ethereum-based. As a result, the majority of markets accept Ether as a valid payment method. To purchase Ether, you must first open an account with a crypto exchange and then transfer the cryptocurrency to your blockchain wallet.

You can connect your wallet to the NFT marketplace account after you have enough funds. Following that, you can now purchase NFT whenever you wish.

Buying NFT

This is the last step in the NFT purchase process. After you've financed your wallet and account, the purchase procedure is simple. On most NFT marketplaces, the auction option is accessible. In this case, you can place your bid. After then, you must wait a certain amount of time to see if the component has arrived. It's possible that an auction will take many days to conclude. If you actually want to own that piece of art, you'll have to outbid the highest bidder.

Purchasing an NFT in the secondary market, on the other hand, is recommended. This is due to the fact that when you put it up for sale on another site, the resale value is rather high. It does, however, have significant drawbacks. In any case, predicting how the NFT will be judged is challenging. Demand might grow or dip at any time.

Now let's look at how to make and sell NFTs on various platforms.

How to Create and Sell NFTs

When it comes to selling NFT, you have two alternatives. To begin, you can buy an existing NFT piece and then resell it on a different platform. Second, you have the option of creating your own NFTs. Then put them up for auction and sell them on other sites. The technique for acquiring NFTs has already been discussed.

How Are NFTs Created?

Creating NFT is, in fact, a pretty basic and straightforward procedure. To do so, you'll need to register with a marketplace that allows you to create NFTs. Users may purchase, sell, and even generate NFTs on marketplaces like Opensea or Rarible. The finest thing is that the ERC-721 coins may be created without any prior understanding of blockchain or cryptographic hashing.

Your image, video, 3D models, or any other item will be converted into NFTs via the platform. It's not the same as asset tokenization. In order for an NFT to be useful, the media must be linked in some way. The reputation of an artist is what gives an NFT its worth.

How Much Does It Cost?

Some platforms will often charge you a nominal fee for creating NFTs. In Opensea, however, there are no charges associated with creating an NFT. Only a one-time gas cost is required. This is a one-time cost that must be paid when you make your first NFT. The rest is completely free. You'll need "gas" to produce the tokens if the marketplace uses Ethereum NFTs.

The price of Ethereum gas varies according on the network. Greater will be the gas price if more individuals are working on the network. It's best to test it out over the weekend when there are less people on the network.

Who Can Make An NFT?

There are no restrictions on who may manufacture an NFT or gain access to the marketplace. Everyone is welcome to attend. An account is all that is required to buy or sell NFTs. Buying is a lot easier procedure than selling. This is due to the value that the token provides. When you're making your own NFTs, though, the value isn't the same.

Not everyone can go out and construct an NFT and expect a decent return on their investment. It's a little like how real-life artists operate. It is more difficult to sell if you are not well-known.

Hidden fees, on the other hand, might grow rather complicated on many sites. Hidden costs might equal to more tokens than you first receive in sales. In this instance, you'll have to sell your tokens at a loss. It is advised to conduct extensive study on the platforms. Before you start minting your NFTs, you may build a fanbase.

The Process of Selling NFTs

It's time to figure out how to sell NFT from your collections. To sell NFT, log in to your account. You must locate the item in your collections. Once you've found them, you must click on them. It will then display a "sell" button.

You may now select this option by clicking it. It will transport you to another page where you may specify the auction's pricing and terms.

In each marketplace, the method is slightly different. If you sell your NFT, one of the common tokens you will receive is ether, also known as ERC-20. Platforms such as Opensea charge a royalty fee. You may earn a commission on every unique item that is sold.

Chapter 14
Future of the NFTs

NFTs are rapidly expanding. They have the potential to cause a paradigm change in the digital world. They may accomplish this by establishing a strong online market for digital producers and investors, as well as multiple methods to secure their work. This is extremely beneficial to digital creators and should not be neglected. The likelihood of success of digital assets such as NFTs must be determined. This is conceivable once they are exchanged in fiat money or the legal structure accepts virtual currencies.

NFTs have the potential to be a useful weapon in the battle against identity theft. However, it is still in its infancy. Its principal application domains are primarily restricted to the bitcoin community. Experts believe that they will develop and spread rapidly in the future. There are two possibilities for the future. Either a highly controlled, disruptive digital market that skyrockets with the goal of protecting virtual copyrights. Another forecast involves an asset that suffers the same fate as numerous cryptocurrencies and bursts.

NFTs depict a lack of permanence. This poses an ecological problem. It is evident that artists are eager to participate in the NFT ecosystem. They are prepared to do so in order to profit from their works of art. However, the selling and acquisition of such tokenized artwork raises issues about the legal ambiguity surrounding its legality. It also raises a number of legal issues. This involves the enforcement of copyright and NFT holders' rights. Another issue is the creator's and holder's responsibility. Other issues include the applicability of several other intersecting laws and the expiration of the copyright holder's rights after the first sale. People who engage in digital transactions with NFTs should be aware of the dangers and risks involved. However, the numerous advantages afforded for the protection of digital works of art cannot be overlooked.

Summary

Non-Fungible Token adoption is still lacking widespread approval throughout the world. NFTs have the potential to offer up new and intriguing avenues for commercializing works of art in the digital realm. However, the adoption of these digital assets in the mainstream art market is crucial. A well-balanced legal regulatory framework is required for its successful operation.

Hope that this book gave a clear picture of what the world of NFTs is? So, comfort yourself with these concepts and try to explore more as you learn more about it.

Good luck.

Be loving & be smiling.

Take care.

- **Vicky V. Choudhary**

References

Wang, Qin & Li, Rujia & Wang, Qi & Chen, Shiping. (2021).
Non-Fungible Token (NFT): Overview, Evaluation,
Opportunities and Challenges.
https://www.researchgate.net/publication/351656444_Non-
Fungible_Token_NFT_Overview_Evaluation_Opportunitie
s_and_Challenges

Yashika Nagpal. Non-Fungible Tokens (NFT's): The Future of
Digital Collectibles, 4 (5) IJLMH Page 758 - 767 (2021),
DOI: https://doij.org/10.10000/IJLMH.111984

Nadini, M., Alessandretti, L., Di Giacinto, F. et al. Mapping the
NFT revolution: market trends, trade networks, and visual
features. Sci Rep 11, 20902 (2021).
https://doi.org/10.1038/s41598-021-00053-8

Ante, Lennart. The non-fungible token (NFT) market and its
relationship with Bitcoin and Ethereum (June 6, 2021).

Available at SSRN: https://ssrn.com/abstract=3861106 or

http://dx.doi.org/10.2139/ssrn.3861106

Regner, Ferdinand & Schweizer, André & Urbach, Nils. (2019).
NFTs in Practice – Non-Fungible Tokens as Core
Component of a Blockchain-based Event Ticketing
Application.
https://www.researchgate.net/publication/336057493_NFTs
_in_Practice_-_Non-
Fungible_Tokens_as_Core_Component_of_a_Blockchain-
based_Event_Ticketing_Application/citation/download

Goushal, Shreyansh. (2021). A Deep Dive into Non-Fungible
Tokens (NFTs) and Its Correlation with the price of Bitcoin
and Ethereum. GJRA - Global Journal for Research
Analysis. Volume - 10, Issue - 08, August- 2021, PRINT
ISSN No. 2277 - 8160 • DOI : 10.36106/gjra
https://www.worldwidejournals.com/global-journal-for-
research-analysis-GJRA/article/a-deep-dive-into-non-

fungible-tokens-nfts-and-its-correlation-with-the-price-of-

bitcoin-and-ethereum/MjEwNjM=/?is=1&b1=29&k=8

Clear Tax. (2022, January 13). NFT, Non Fungible Token –

Definition, Why NFTs are Valuable, Uses & Features of

NFTs. https://cleartax.in/s/nft-non-fungible-token

Portion Blog. (2021). The History of NFTs & How They Got

Started? https://blog.portion.io/the-history-of-nfts-how-

they-got-started/

Piven, Ben. (March 26, 2021). NFT craze: Why are non-fungible

tokens all the rage? Aljazeera.

https://www.aljazeera.com/economy/2021/3/26/nft-craze-

why-are-non-fungible-tokens-all-the-rage

Schiller, David & Skillicorn, Chris. (2021, February 18). What Is a

Non-Fungible Token? A Beginner's Guide. Enjin.

https://enjin.io/blog/nft-beginners-

guide?utm_source=google_ads&utm_medium=cpc&utm_c

ampaign=IN_generic_nft&gclid=Cj0KCQiAi9mPBhCJAR

IsAHchl1wH0n5d3cLM-

kxKs0iVZCxoIeQqREmL461Tx2C67bG-

XFVHdBkpwggaAojcEALw_wcB

Iredale, Gwyneth. (2021, March 24). The Difference Between

Fungible And Non-Fungible Tokens. 101 Blockchains.

https://101blockchains.com/fungible-vs-non-fungible-

tokens/

Anwar, Hasib. (2021, April 11). How To Buy And Sell NFTs? 101

Blockchains. https://101blockchains.com/buy-and-sell-nfts/

Cointelegraph. (n.d.). The NFT marketplace: How to buy and sell

nonfungible tokens?

https://cointelegraph.com/nonfungible-tokens-for-

beginners/the-nft-marketplace-how-to-buy-and-sell-

nonfungible-tokens

DiLallo, Mathew. (2022, January 22). How to Make an NFT? The

Motley Fool. https://www.fool.com/investing/stock-

market/market-sectors/financials/non-fungible-tokens/how-

to-make-an-nft/